My Healthy Body
Eating

Veronica Ross

Thameside Press

Distributed in the United States by
Smart Apple Media
1980 Lookout Drive
North Mankato, MN 56003

Text by Veronica Ross

ISBN 1-930643-83-7

Library of Congress Control Number 2002 141342

Design: Bean Bog Frag Design
Picture researcher: Terry Forshaw
Consultant: Carol Ballard

Printed in Taiwan

10 9 8 7 6 5 4 3 2 1

Picture acknowledgements:
(T) = Top, (B) = Bottom, (L) = Left, (R) = Right, (C) = Center

All Photography by Claire Paxton with the exception of: 5 © Digital
Vision; 6 (TR), (TCR), (BCR); 7 (TL), (TR), (CR), (BL), (BC); 8 (TL), (TR); 9 (TR),
(CL); 11 (CL), (BL); 12 (TR); 13 (TL), (TCL), (TCR), (BR); 14 (T), (B); 15 (TR), (C),
(BL); 17 (TR), (TC), (TCR), (BCL), 19 (TC), (TR); Chrysalis Images 20 ©
Bubbles/Ian West; 22 (BL) Chrysalis Images; 23 © Corbis/Earl &
Nazima Kowall; 24 (T) Chrysalis Images; 25 © Wellcome Photo
Library/Anthea Sieveking; 26 © Photo Disc/Ryan Mcvay; 27 (T) ©
Bubbles/Chris Miles, (B) Bubbles/Richard Yard; 29
(B) Chrysalis Images.

Contents

Why do I eat?

Everyone needs to eat. Food helps you to stay healthy and gives the energy you need to work and play. Food also helps protect from illness and makes you grow.

If you don't eat for some hours, you will soon begin to feel very hungry.

Your body uses energy when you work and play, even when you're painting pictures!

You should try to eat three healthy meals each day.

A balanced diet

You need to eat lots of
different foods to stay healthy.
A well-balanced diet includes
different types of foods that give
you all the goodness you need.

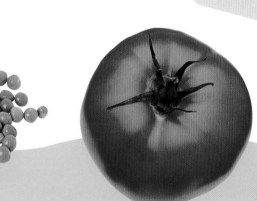

How many of these
foods can you name?
How many do you like to eat?

Fruit and vegetables are very good for you.

Your "diet" is the food and drink that you eat and drink every day.

Foods for growth

Meat, fish, milk, eggs, cheese, nuts, beans, and cereals help you to grow. They also keep your body in good working order.

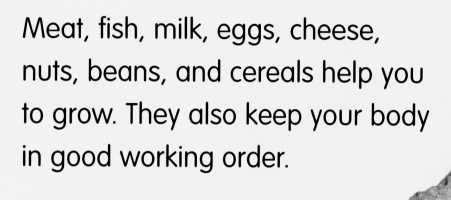

Eggs make you grow strong. Eat one for breakfast about twice a week!

Growth foods help to repair broken bones.

The foods shown on these pages will build your muscles, bones, and teeth.

Energy foods

Rice, bread, cereals, potatoes, and pasta give you energy and help keep you warm. You should try to eat some of these foods at every main meal.

Fruit also gives you energy.

Start the day with a breakfast of toast or cereal for a burst of energy.

If you play lots of sport, you will need to eat extra energy foods.

Fatty and oily

You only need to eat small amounts of fatty foods to keep fit and well. Fat is found in many foods, such as chocolate, butter, cheese, milk, and vegetable oil.

Foods such as French fries and tortillas may contain a lot of fat.

Try not to eat too many chocolate bars, cakes, and cookies.

If you're feeling hungry between meals, try to eat an apple or a banana instead of a cookie.

13

Food for health

Different foods do different jobs. Vegetables and fruit give you healthy skin and blood, and help cuts to heal. Milk, cheese, and yogurt give you calcium, which keeps your bones strong.

Dark green vegetables, such as broccoli, are especially good for you.

Fish are packed with goodness. They will help you to grow.

A glass of milk every day will help keep your teeth healthy.

Oranges help your body fight off coughs and colds.

Fantastic fiber

Some foods, such as pasta, whole-wheat bread, and vegetables, contain fiber. Fiber helps your body use the food that you eat.

Foods rich in fiber make you feel very full.

Pasta, lentils, brown rice, whole-wheat bread, fruit, and vegetables contain fiber.

Fiber is found in plants such as wheat.

Drink up

You could survive for some weeks or even months without food, but for much less time without water. All the parts of your body need water.

Your body needs about four pints of water a day.

You need to drink more when it is hot. This is because you sweat more in hot weather, and you must replace the water you lose.

Water is found in fruit and vegetables as well as drinks.

Being a vegetarian

Vegetarians are people who do not eat meat. If you decide to become a vegetarian, you should eat a wide variety of fruit and vegetables, as well as beans, nuts, milk, and cheese. These foods will help give you the goodness you need.

Many restaurants offer vegetarian food.

This meal of rice, salad, and stuffed pepper can be as healthy as a meal that contains meat.

Make a picnic packed with tasty vegetarian food.

Some vegetarians do not like the taste of meat. Others believe that eating animals is wrong.

Food, fabulous food

Food keeps us healthy, but eating a delicious meal is also very enjoyable! That's why we eat special foods when we celebrate birthdays, weddings, or festivals. What are your favorite foods?

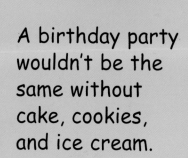

A birthday party wouldn't be the same without cake, cookies, and ice cream.

A wedding
feast in Korea.

A large meal can stay in your
stomach for more than three hours.

Food allergies

Some people are allergic to certain foods. Milk, eggs, shellfish, strawberries, peanuts, and chocolate are some foods that can cause a rash or stomachache.

Chocolate may give some people a headache.

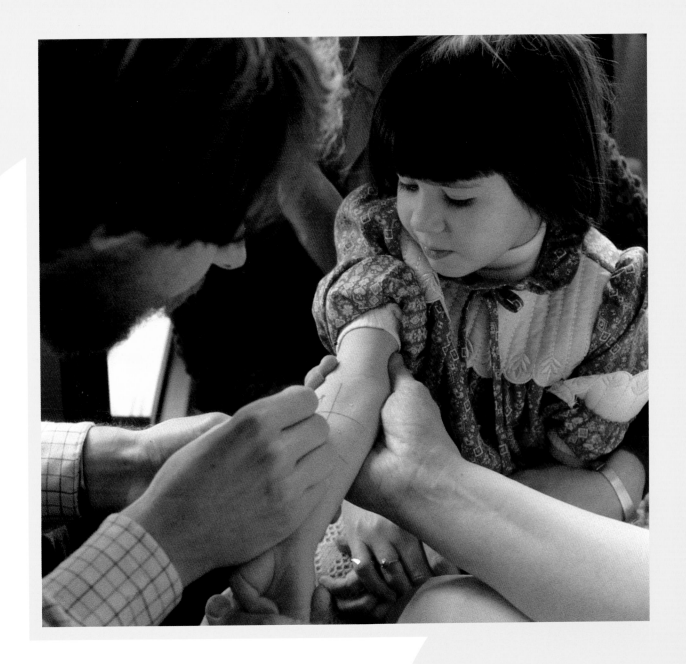

If you think you have a food allergy, your doctor may give you special tests to find out which food makes you feel unwell.

Some foods have chemicals in them which give the food extra color or taste. These may make some people feel sick.

preparing food

It's important to make sure that your hands are clean before you eat or pick up food. Keep fish, meat, cheese, and milk in the fridge. Throw away food that is past its sell-by date.

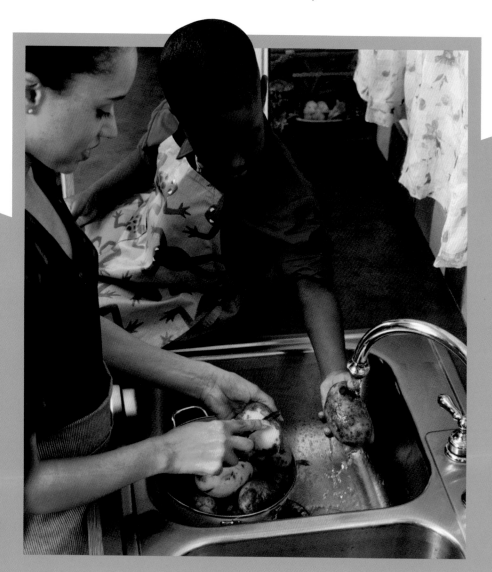

Always wash fruit and vegetables before you eat them.

Put on an apron before you start cooking.

When you have finished, wash your hands and clean up!

Do not leave food uncovered, especially in hot weather.

27

Bad habits

Fast foods, such as French fries, hamburgers, and donuts, are often high in fat, sugar, and salt. If you ate only this type of food all the time, you would soon become very unhealthy.

Too many sweet foods and high-sugar drinks can make your teeth decay.

Burgers and fries taste great, but they are often full of fat. Try eating more of other healthier foods.

If you eat too much food at one time, you might feel sick!

Words to remember

allergy

A reaction to food or other things, such as dust or pollen.

blood

The red liquid that flows around your body.

bones

The hard parts inside your body that make up your skeleton.

calcium

A main substance helping to form your bones.

decay

To go bad or to rot.

energy

The power you need to be able to work and play without feeling tired.

muscles
Bundles of soft, stretchy fibers inside your body that make you move.

protect
To look after.

repair
To mend.

tortillas
Flat, round cornmeal pancakes, often with fillings.

sweat
Water that comes from your skin when you are very hot.

whole-wheat bread
Bread that is made with the whole grain.

Index